The Great House

by Lily Browne
illustrated by Xiangyi Mo

Harcourt
SCHOOL PUBLISHERS

Printed in China

ISBN 10: 0-15-350395-5
ISBN 13: 978-0-15-350395-5

Ordering Options
ISBN 10: 0-15-350331-9 (Grade 1 Below-Level Collection)
ISBN 13: 978-0-15-350331-3 (Grade 1 Below-Level Collection)
ISBN 10: 0-15-357421-6 (package of 5)
ISBN 13: 978-0-15-357421-4 (package of 5)

3 4 5 6 7 8 9 10   468   15 14 13 12 11 10 09 08

James was building
a house.

"Can I help make the
house?" said Jen.

"This cloth can be the walls," said Jen. "They can be red."

"I'll make the roof," said James. The house grew tall.

"I'll turn over this box," said Jen. "It can be the table."

"Let's have a flag for the house," said James.

"I'll make a path," said
Jen. "It will look nice
and welcoming."

"We made a house!" said James and Jen.

"I made a pie!" said Dad.

"Let's eat the pie in the house," said James.

"This is a good house," said Mom.

"This is a *great* house," said Dad.

"This is a great *pie*!" said Jen.

"We have to go in now,"
said Mom and Dad.

"Make a pie tomorrow
too, Dad!" said Jen.

"You can eat it in our
house with us," said James.